Harness is a *verb:*

> *to control and make use of (natural resources), especially to produce energy*

HARNESS precious time and FREE your mind so you can thrive. Become even more present, efficient, and liberated from anything that runs inside you and your organization that steals your energy, well-being, engagement, creativity and productivity.

D1594485

Fast Reads/Luna Madre™ Publishing
Santa Barbara, California

Harness Time and Free Your Mind

Author: Linda Newlin
Editors: Barbie Jones and Johnny Ruffin
Cover Design: Cecilia Martini Muth, CC Design, Santa Barbara
ISBN: 979-8-9854869-1-9
Library of Congress: 2023916121

www.HarnessTimeandFreeYourMind.com

Copyright © 2023

Table of Contents

Why do I write, coach and teach?

Because I want to continue to cultivate presence, freedom and peace in my own life and help others to create what they want and need in their lives. I want to create more energy so I can do my life's purpose and enjoy this one precious life I have.

I wrote this book because I hear every day, everywhere I go, the exact same thing:

"I don't have enough time."

I realized many years ago that I had this running inside me and it was stealing my mental and emotional energy. I was always racing and had difficulty staying still even when I was fully stopped. This impacted many more things than I could imagine.

This process and practices have changed my life and I hope it changes yours. I want you to gain what you want and need right now to shift what is getting in the way of you being more present, expressing fully who you are, living congruently and thriving in all areas of your life.

I believe that being a great coach requires that you continue to be a great learner. I continually seek new methodologies grounded in applied neuroscience to help my clients create sustainable change. Thank you to Dr. Irena O'Brien at the Neuro Science School new research that influences how I have presented the science behind this methodology.

I created a new FAST READS publishing imprint out of the desire to be congruent with what I write and teach.

Keep it short and on point!

This book contains valuable tools and transformative practices grounded in science, positive psychology, 3 brains coaching, and 30 years of experience coaching global leaders, teams and individuals.

You will learn and practice how to:

Gain power over that which runs inside you that consumes your TIME and ENERGY so you can thrive

Free your mind to make space for more positivity, innovation, possibilities, joy and peace

Transform self-limiting thoughts, stories and old patterns of behavior that limit your productivity, ease and self confidence

Release the past and live more in the now

Improve your focus and efficiency

Manage your attention more effectively

Take inspired action toward your desired vision

Become more authentic and congruent

Improve your sleep and well-being

Increase your presence to lead and live your life more effectively

Learn valuable new research that you can apply to change your brain and your life

Shift from victim mindset to creator

Move out of rescuing to coaching

Work with your biology to rewire the brain and create sustainable change

Embrace the practice of experimenting

What would you do if you had more time?

HARNESS TIME and FREE YOUR MIND

What is time?

There are many answers to this question, however the objective definition most of us understand is that time is measured by a clock that is equal and unchanging for all individuals.

We all have 24 hours per day.

Time perception is often described as fast or slow.

For some, time seems slower when sad events occur and speeds up when happy events happen.

It is an intangible element of our modern daily life as it organizes events in the order of their occurrence and flow.

The concept of time has been studied in many fields including philosophy, physics and mathematics. The definition of time differs slightly in all these fields of study.

Throughout history, mankind has tried to measure time with varies methods. It started with the seasons.

It was sensation based. Is it hot or cold?

Ancient Egyptians described time as the **disappearance of energy**.

Time is an extremely deep concept and yet it is clear that one **cannot unwind, renew or trade** it.

Time is the most precious commodity we all seek to gain more of.

There are many time management systems out there that are designed to help you answer part of this question. They can help you institute some strategic changes to scheduling, prioritizing and managing your calendar using technological solutions.

However, I've discovered even more profound ways to gain precious time. It involves identifying and letting go of the things that are running inside your mind and your organization that are robbing you of your time, focus, vitality, presence and creativity. And it is about your presence and energy.

When you work through the book you will become aware of the many things that are running inside you that have a huge impact on your ability to thrive and not just survive. These saboteurs, as I call them, include things like: insecurity, imposter syndrome, inner critique, ruminating, procrastination, fear, judgments, self-doubt, analysis paralysis, resentments and distractions to name a few.

Some are more significant in their impact for you. Many interfere with your ability to be present, have quality sleep, peace of mind, and perform at your ideal level physically, emotionally and intellectually. This impacts your effectiveness in life, work, relationships as well as your health and happiness.

Welcome to Harness Time and Free Your Mind!

It's been nearly a decade since I wrote the book *Drop It: A Coach's Secret to Productivity, Presence and Possibility*. In that time, I have worked with leaders and their teams in global organizations that are working more hours than ever. They are struggling to manage efficiently and sustain themselves in the current reality of "doing more with less," globalization, working from home, back-to-back meetings, hundreds of emails, 24/7 communication demands and managing their multi-generational teams remotely.

They are also trying to balance work, manage their careers, produce more results and have time for their home life.

Needless to say, the sustainability of our health and relationships are also in question. Divorce rates are hitting 60% in some countries and stress related diseases are increasing at an alarming rate in our work force and communities.

Organizations are spending billions of dollars on EAP programs to support people through this current reality.

My passion and purpose in life is to remove the suffering of others. Thus, my desire to continue to bring forth change tools that truly help people and organizations to gain what they want and need. We all need more energy.

I am grateful to the scientists who continue to discover and share their knowledge about how our 3 brains work and what we can do to shift thoughts and behaviors more quickly and sustain behavior changes that we make. My study and coaching in this arena have helped me to refine and enhance the effective Drop It™ methodology for individuals and organizations who are desiring an effective program and process to harness time, free their mind, enhance their leadership presence and create high performing teams.

In coaching thousands of leaders and their teams for three decades, I've discovered that one of the most limiting factors in being more productive, innovative, present and available for more possibilities is the inability to eliminate and free oneself from the many things they **hang on to.**

This includes: unproductive beliefs, ineffective programmed self-limiting behaviors, grudges, past hurts, perfectionism, distractions, stories they tell themselves and the ever sabotaging "shoulds" as they tirelessly add more and more to their lists of things to do; hanging themselves literally over time.

This creates a survival mode of being.

You cannot thrive if you continue to run the old programming, outdated strategies and beliefs that were modeled in your early life and passed down through the generations before you.

If you keep hanging on to the past, you will do harm to yourself and others you care about.

How can you stop this destructive way of thinking, living and being to do things differently?

You have to choose to move beyond surviving by releasing the old hurts, programs, and beliefs so that you can install new ways of being, new beliefs and new energy that creates positive and lasting change.

This program is born out of the life changing experiences of my clients who have discovered the power of this process.

Being a catalyst for change is what I do as a coach and I feel fortunate to have worked with organizations, leaders and individuals who need and want to change the way they work and how they live in order to gain the energy to sustain themselves in this challenging global environment.

I have never met anyone, including myself, who doesn't need to change something about how they think, act or feel.

Leaders are pressed to be more productive, increase employee engagement through their presence and create possibilities for greater employee retention.

The challenge to thrive, maintain balance and create sustainable lives and organizations is increasingly more difficult and the practice of managing change has been to add more as opposed to delete.

While change may require that you add new activities or stop doing others, I believe that one of the secrets to gaining freedom that has a much greater impact on productivity, presence and possibility is when you can learn and practice DROP IT.

Yes, **DROP IT works!**

"I can't believe how quickly my mojo returned after doing this. I've been unable to show up at my best for the past few years. I didn't know the impact being made redundant from my last role was having until now.

This released all the negative energy I had been hanging on to that was sabotaging my ability to present to the senior leadership team with confidence and ease.

This is amazing. Thank you!"

~ Peter

Whatever it is that drains your

ENERGY and TIME,

holds you hostage to the past,

runs over and over through your mind,

makes you sick and tired

or creates guilt and self-punishment

is what you want to discover and name.

Then you can

calculate the costs and tell the truth

so that you can exercise your will

to choose freedom and

learn to Empty Out and Drop It.

This is a process that will enhance your

effectiveness, presence, relationships and

your health and well-being.

Scientists have estimated that we may have more than 50,000 thoughts per day (most are unconscious).

Some are positive, productive and valuable. And many are not.

There is a Rwandan Proverb that says:

"You can outrun that which runs after you, but you can't outrun that which runs inside you."

What is running inside your mind now that you are aware of?

What keeps you up at night?

What is running inside your organization and inside your employee's minds right now?

In this moment, if you had to guess, how much time do you spend running repetitive and negative internal dialogues that chew up your valuable time and energy?

What negative scenarios, stories, worries, limiting beliefs are sabotaging your focus, confidence, presence and creativity?

Take a quick guess on how much time is being spent in your organization on all that runs within people's minds at this time and how the past may still be operating within the culture? (complaining, drama, fear and stories people retell)

What would be possible if you could harness all that time and energy and focus on more innovation, creativity and growth?

Your head brain works like a computer in many ways. It has many programs that run within you. Some are positive, and some that have been installed are counter-productive to your well-being and effectiveness. And you can change it!

You can identify and reprogram that which is running inside you and your organization. This DROP IT 2.0 process will help create a different internal experience that directly impacts your work and your relationships.

Leaders are facing increased expectations to be more present and authentic in order to empower and engage their employees for higher retention and productivity. Individuals are seeking sustainability and freedom in their lives.

You can reprogram your brain and find freedom. If you choose to engage your free will choice and take action.

Imagine what will be possible when you free your mind

What will it feel like?

What will be possible with more peace and presence?

What new feelings and energy might you have?

How will you be showing up differently at home and at work?

What self-care will you be engaged in more consistently?

How will your relationships be?

What would your quality of sleep be?

HARNESS TIME and FREE YOUR MIND

WORKING WITH YOUR BIOLOGY TO CREATE LASTING CHANGE

CHANGE YOUR BEHAVIOR, CHANGE YOUR BRAIN

CHANGE YOUR BRAIN, CHANGE YOUR BEHAVIOR

Working WITH the body and the science of human behavior has been a game changer for me and my clients.

As a coach and leadership consultant, I am hired to help my clients create sustainable change that has a high impact and a greater return on the investment of money and time.

In the last 30 years, I've learned that changing human behavior requires that we work with how we are wired to operate and use the new scientific discoveries in neurobiology and neuroscience to implement tools and methodologies that work to create the lasting changes we desire.

Scientists are finding out new things everyday about how our amazing complex brains work. What we thought was true 10 years ago is no longer accurate due to new research and technology that allows information to come to light that helps us to understand how to work with and not against our biology.

Your brain likes to GAIN. It does not like to lose.

When you choose to focus on what you will gain by making a behavior change that you desire, it is easier for your brain to organize itself around the anticipated positive impact/gain. The systems align together to move TOWARD your desired outcome.

Interestingly, it would appear that the weight loss industry has made billions of dollars off this biological fact. When a person loses weight, the brain says, "NO, NO, we don't like losing, we must gain it back and gain some more."

The binary GAIN/LOSE dynamic seems to be a function of the brain. Another example is when someone "loses" a love interest. Even if it wasn't a positive experience, if they feel they've lost that love, they may find themselves wanting to gain that person back even if it was unhealthy or not ideal.

This also validates why visioning in a certain way works better.

The brain likes to focus on what it will GAIN in the future and it wants to move TOWARD the payoffs it feels and desires. This needs to include the steps it will take to get what you are envisioning.

The brain does not know the difference between rehearsing and doing, so athletes have used this for decades to practice in their minds. You can practice new behaviors in the safety of your mind first before you do it for real.

You will learn more about visioning that produces results and how to use your brain's desire to GAIN more effectively.

And remember that the brain hears what we say, think and feel and responds accordingly, so if you say "I can't", you will not be able to do what it is you are attempting to do. I remember experimenting with my young son when he wanted to do a new physical behavior that he'd never done before. When he said "I can't", he could not do it. When he said, "I can", he could. It is so simple and yet we don't use this reality for our own good in more areas than just physical.

We have the possibility to create more than what we imagine.

Once you have done something "unimaginable" you then have a new standard of what is possible. I remember walking on 2000-degree hot coals a few years ago. It was incredible!

AND you must do this with a trained facilitator!

I had to believe I could do it without getting burned. I had to overcome the limiting beliefs and thoughts that were in my mind. This experience is a reference point for me and my brain.

I now know that I am capable of doing things beyond my limited programmed beliefs that I had carried around with me.

If you're not into heat, there are other "mind over matter" practices like cold water therapy to reprogram your brain which are also beneficial to your health and wellbeing.

RESIST

YOUR

RESISTANCE!

Notice if you have any resistance arising right now.

Why do humans resist?

One reason is because we learned to resist by our early childhood experiences and we have also been programmed in our DNA from the seven generations before us (Epigenetics).

Your brain is built on past experience.

Those unconscious patterned responses, thoughts and feelings continue to run inside your body and mind until you become aware that these are sabotaging you and you name them, make a conscious choice to empty out and delete the old programs.

In this book, you will learn to identify your resistance so you can choose to free your body and mind of that which no longer serves you.

When you practice new behaviors, feelings, thoughts and experiences, you will create a new positive recent past for the brain to shape itself around and operate differently.

And, your body is not just a one brain taxi.

HEAD

The CONSULTANT

Objective: To predict the future correctly by using stored history

HEART

The WE Brain

Objective: Belong, feel loved, care about others and apply values to the greater whole

GUT

The ME Brain

Objective: Survive, satisfy desires, get my own needs met

Each brain has a purpose and when you understand them and work WITH them, you can create and gain more integration, peace, presence and make better, faster decisions. You can also improve your relationships dramatically.

Your gut brain forms first in the womb. It is your ME brain. Its main function is to protect you, keep you alive, get your needs met, satisfy your desires. It wants you to get what you want and drives your need/desire to survive.

The heart brain is your WE brain. It drives your desire to connect with others, care, nurture, belong and feel loved. It is the home of your values and what you care about for the greater whole. These two brains are action centers.

The head brain's objective is to predict the future correctly. It acts more like a consultant. It is a resource for accessing data, stores the history of your prior decisions, experiences, and learning. It is where the awareness of time resides (past, present, future.)

When the gut brain or heart brain can't decide, it may consult the head brain to give data to the inquiry about what to do based on past memories and information the head brain has stored.

The head brain can unlearn old programs and patterned behaviors and it can learn new ways of being and operating. When you learn new things, the head brain can offer updated positive alternatives for decision making, thoughts and beliefs to apply to life's choices and feeling states of being.

Like a computer, the head brain accesses the most recent stored memory and information.

If you have been taking positive actions toward your desired outcome, your brain registers this information and wires a new neuropathway that runs a new program called "I can change and create a new reality for myself."

As you think about the head brain being a consultant to you, what would you want it to provide to you in terms of messages, data, thoughts, images and states of being?

There are some old sayings that may be useful here. "You are what you eat and what you think." Or some might say it this way, "garbage in - garbage out."

You shape yourself around what you hear, see, feel, say, do and what you think about all that.

I remember learning 35 years ago about the Myers Briggs Type Indicator and what scientists were sharing about the brain.

The head brain is continually doing 2 things:

1. Perceiving information
2. Deciding what to do with the information it perceives.

What information do you expose yourself to?

What setting are you living and working in and what information and feeling states are generated there?

What is the emotional energy of your relationships and the people you interact with?

What thoughts do you choose to fill your head with?

In this moment, think about what you expose yourself to in terms of "input" on any given day. What messages from the media, TV, film, conversations, books, music, etc.

How is that serving your desired state of being? Is that input helping you gain more time, health, presence, efficiency and confidence in your ability to create what you desire and need?

The difference between creators of change and non-creators is one exercises their free will choice and applies knowledge and tools to change and grow. Creators choose what they watch, read and who they interact with as much as possible.

It is true that making one small shift can lead to great long-term significant change over time.

Imagine what would be possible if you chose to input positive, inspiring media, or did something fun or nourishing for your brain and body? (learn a new instrument, language or dance)

What do you imagine would happen if you started validating yourself for the things you did well in each day and stopped focusing on what you didn't get done?

As you can tell, already I will be posing evocative questions throughout this journey. That is what coaches do.

It is also my goal to teach you how to enhance your own self coaching capacities within this process.

Right now, in the world, one of the biggest challenges humans have is managing their attention and focus. Time thieves are everywhere. Media, technology, drama, repetitive conversations with ourselves and others to name a few.

How can you manage your thoughts and attention more effectively?

Attention is something that happens with or without you. Your mind will wander and pay attention to whatever is captivating.

One way to gain control of your attention is to breathe and center yourself. Be still. Feel your sensations.

A Buddhist Lama told me think of the breath as the horse. The mind is the jockey. In order to have power over where the mind is taking you, use your breath! Have you heard about screen apnea? People forget to breathe when on screens.

BREATHING IS KEY TO BEING PRESENT

When you breathe and center yourself in your body, you become more present in this moment. Being fully embodied is another super power for life. It is one of the key ways to become present and embody the power within yourself to choose how you want to be.

When you are centered, you have access to resources beyond your limited mind and thinking patterns.

You are able to take conscious inspired action that produces what you want to gain.

Conscious breathing supports transformation and presence.

I could write an entire book on the power of using breathing as a transformation tool and resource. For now, I encourage you to practice this as you embark on the inner work.

Take a slow deep breath now. (Inhale into your belly). Like a balloon when it fills with air, the belly expands, then release. Breathing through the nose is most effective for calming the nervous system and focusing. Please take another deep breath. And one more.

Feel the sensations you are aware of after taking a few deep breaths.

If one of your intentions is to free your mind, note the power of focusing and taking 3 deep breaths consciously.

When you focus on your body, you become more present. You are not thinking about the future or the past. Remember your head brain desires to predict the future, which is why you likely default to **thinking** more than **feeling** your body sensations or choosing to breathe consciously to bring yourself to the moment you're in. Simply put, **BE WHERE YOU ARE.**

Presence is a gift you give yourself and others.

You are in the present when you are fully in the moment.

People know when you are somewhere else (even if they don't say anything to you.) This can breed disappointment and disconnection over time.

> It's important to know that when you are truly PRESENT, people will perceive that you are spending 2-3 times longer with them.

This is another way to gain TIME. BE MORE PRESENT!!!

Intention + Action = Results

People judge you on your actions and results, not on your intentions.

If you say you want to be more PRESENT with those you care about and you are on your phone when you're with them, you are not being present.

If you are thinking about what you still need to do later while trying to listen to someone, you are not listening.

If you are thinking about what you're going to say next, you are not listening either.

Intentions can be your hopes, wishes, desires and goals.

When you set a goal for yourself and you intend to achieve it can be very helpful to use these questions to create results.

"Will this action help me gain what I say I want?"

"Is this thought/behavior in service of my vision?

Often people will say to me, "I don't know what I really want." I say, "What if you did know, what would you want?" I just know what I don't want."

"WHAT IF, YOU DID KNOW?"

Becoming clear on what you want instead of what you don't want is important because of the way the brain works. Your brain likes to gain and it is motivated to move toward the desired shift. It's not helpful to try and do less of a bad behavior.

Let's say you are defensive and reactive when you receive feedback. You would like to be less defensive. The brain doesn't see the real gain in that.

What do you want instead?

To be present, open and receive feedback as a gift.

I want to be calm, centered and accept the information as data to consider and behavior to adjust so I can shift to be even more effective.

Being specific about your desired state and outcome helps your brain to focus on the gain and predict the new future state.

Conscious breathing is also helpful when you want to gain clarity as it quiets the internal churn and negative unconscious mind so you can connect with what you truly want.

We know that the body doesn't lie.

You can access the wisdom of your body by asking your head, heart and gut what they want.

Breathe now and ask your gut what it wants. Remember that it's your ME brain, so it will often want things to help you thrive, be satisfied, feel positive physical sensations.

The heart brain wants to belong, connect, be loved.

My first book *"The Inner Traveler's Guidebook to Moyo: Discovering the Power of Listening to Your Own Heart"* was written after I experienced the clarity and gift of having a dialogue with my heart that changed my life.

Since then, I've been building a relationship with all my three brains to find clarity, balance, insights and traction.

Each brain has different wants and needs. Your gut brain needs safety. Your heart brain wants connection. Building a relationship with all 3 brains requires taking time to listen. Let's practice listening to your heart brain now.

I encourage people to stop, breathe and sit quietly. Imagine you're breathing in and out of your heart like it is your lung. Inhale it expands, exhale it contracts. Take a few deep breaths focusing on your heart. Some people put their hand on their chest as they imagine connecting with their heart brain.

Then ask your heart what it wants. Keep breathing and listen for the message that will arise.

Receive whatever it says.

Sometimes it's a big surprise and something you may or may not have known was living inside you.

Sometimes it is a very familiar "calling" that you have suppressed since you were young.

Sometimes it's a deep emotional desire we haven't received.

It's important to know that just because you hear what your heart wants, doesn't mean that you must act on it or understand it right away.

The first time I asked my heart it said, "songwriting." I was caught off guard and blew it off as "I don't have time to do that."

You know the quote, "Don't die with the music inside you." Or the Thomas Aquinas quote, "Bring forth that which is inside you or it will destroy you." My heart was spot on and the songs and book I wrote changed not only my life.

Another time I asked my heart what it wanted, it replied, "To live in Italy."

In my experience, I can now say that my heart knows what my path is, what will make me truly happy and it helps me to bring forth the gifts and talents I buried inside myself.

When I am happy, I feel like I have more time.

There is a lot of research on the value of being happy and that a company's retention is directly impacted by how many happy bosses they have managing their precious people.

The pursuit of health and happiness will save you time!

I've also recently heard that science is exploring the question of whether the eyes tell the brain what to see, or if our mind tells the eyes what to see?

Imagining, visioning, dreaming and goal setting are all forms of providing information for the brain to perceive and then make decisions from.

Companies have used these tools to drive the outcomes they desire around product development, financial goals, culture and values. Visions and goals help you create more traction vs. distraction.

Traction increases with clarity of intentions + action

FOR THE SAKE OF WHAT are you going to learn to manage your thoughts and attention so you can produce the results you want in all areas of your life?

BRAIN SCIENCE AND PRODUCTIVITY

The source of the information contained in this chapter is from my certification in Applied Neuroscience and years of studying the scientific research that supports this change methodology. It is brief summaries of key insights to help you in this journey.

NEUROPLASTICITY

The brain is plastic and can rewire itself based on experience. This means that all behavior change is brain change.

How you can encourage more neuroplasticity:

- You need to have a goal/clear intention/desire.
    a. This accounts for 28% of the variance in behavior change.

- You must put EFFORT into the learning.
    a. If it's easy your brain has already been wired for that.
    b. Learn a new musical instrument, a new language, chess, word games, study anything new.

- You need REPETITION over time.
    a. Practicing performance enhancing techniques.
    b. Change your beliefs.
    c. Other cognitive change strategies you'll learn

The brain is built on past experience. When you do something new, that becomes the recent past. Remember the head brain repeats what it most recently experienced.

Each time you make a change in your beliefs or behavior your brain changes.

MULTI-TASKING

Multi-tasking is an attempt to do two or more tasks at the same time.

MULTI-TASKING IS THE ART

OF MESSING UP A LOT OF THINGS

ALL AT ONCE

Scientists research reveals these important truths:

- The brain can NOT multi task.

- When you think you are multi-tasking, your brain is actually switching tasks very quickly.

- This means that when you are trying to multi-task, the cognitive resources available to both tasks is reduced, resulting in reduced productivity and increased errors.

SOLUTION: If you want to do more in less time, concentrate on one task at a time.

- Scientist's studies show up to a 40% reduction in productivity, efficiency and quality work product when you are not single focused when you are performing work related tasks.

What would you do with 40% more productivity?

A study that looked at distracted driving found that, in addition to making more mistakes, brain recruitment shifted away from the crucial brain areas responsible for visual and spatial processing. The results are similar for other studies around different domains.

Multi-tasking does not work when you are doing important activities (doing your job, driving, operating heavy equipment, thinking strategically, all things that require focus and attention).

You can choose to do more than one thing at a time in other domains that don't require attention/focus and quality output like:

- Walking and listening to a podcast while in nature or in non- dangerous situations
- Cooking and listening to music, podcasts, tv
- Brushing your teeth and doing isometric exercise (Sitting at the wall to strengthen your legs, butt and abs; calf raises)
- Washing dishes and doing calf raises, stretching, etc.

Please note that when you are with other people and you want to be present. Presence means single-focused attention on the other person and the situation. Being right here, right now.

- Multi-tasking is not presence.
- Most people can tell if you're doing something else when you are speaking with them on the phone. How many times have other people said, "You aren't really here." Or you're doing something else while you are engaging with them.

Presence is a felt experience. The body knows when someone is physically there but mentally elsewhere.

INCREASING MOTIVATION THROUGH THE PROGRESS LOOP

1. The single best way to increase motivation is to make progress in meaningful work, no matter how small.

2. This leads to greater creativity and productivity.

3. Your brain feeds on the positive feelings that come from dopamine hits. When you complete a meaningful task successfully, no matter how small, this burst of dopamine fuels the desire to do more. This is the progress loop that increases motivation and increases the probability of success on the next task.

4. If you fail at completing a task, this leads to a drop in dopamine which increases the probability of failure on the next task or procrastination.

SOLUTION FOR INCREASING MOTIVATION AND PROGRESS:

Create a string of successes by breaking down big goals/jobs into small, manageable tasks. The tasks should be small enough for you to succeed at. This will bring the dopamine which increases your desire to do more to get more of it.

Experiment and observe the difference when you start your work day completing things that you've been procrastinating on. Notice what "story" you've been telling yourself about doing this task that you've been delaying doing.

Do not think about the whole big thing like "I have to write a proposal today". Break it down into the first step you can complete and then the next small task until you reach completion. Motivation increases when we're making progress no matter how small the task.

WILLPOWER

Willpower used to be seen as a depleting resource. Recent studies have found that people who are good at resisting temptation report experiencing fewer temptations. Simply put: The people who said they excel at self-control were hardly using it at all. Some interesting things to consider:

1. People who are better at self-control actually enjoy the activities others resist—like healthy eating, studying, or exercising.

2. They make activities more enjoyable by adding a fun component to them, such as going to the gym with a friend. Or choosing a place where they have friends they love and that's the only time they get to hang out.

3. Learn better habits. A healthy eater would not buy a cupcake or walk by a bakery. They might use the self-checkout at grocery stores where there is less candy/sugar to buy. One might have groceries delivered.

4. Experiment with avoiding sugar, wheat/gluten/grains, caffeine and alcohol. Notice what happens to your brain functioning, sleep, focus and energy. If you have positive desirable changes, you can choose to focus on rewiring your brain toward the gains. If you want more vitality, efficiency and concentration then your will use your will to focus on the positive gains to help drive change.

5. Some people just experience fewer temptations and it may be due to genetics. No matter what it may be, notice if your brain wants to use this as an excuse.

STRESS

1. Stress is a state that people experience on a daily basis.

2. It can take your prefrontal cortex offline, essentially cutting off access to thoughtful behavior. This strengthens the amygdala behavior and stress behaviors become reflexive, leading to repetitive knee jerk reactions.

3. When we perceive threat or danger, this part of our brain goes into immediate survival response to save us.

This stress reaction is the state of fight, flight or freeze. The amygdala reacts in .07 seconds. It is the part of our brain that is responsible for our survival instincts. It's called the Amygdala.

Chronic amygdala hijackings (as I call them) and chronic stress also has potential negative health consequences leading to high blood pressure, heart disease, obesity, and diabetes.

Some stress is inevitable, but the negative health and psychological consequences of stress are not inevitable.

SOLUTION:

1. Practice new habits to reduce stress and build your resilience by calming the nervous system:

   a. Breathing
   b. Centering
   c. Meditation and yoga
   d. Exercise and doing things that bring you joy
   e. Healthy eating
   f. Positive thinking
   g. Be in nature

2. Stop multi-tasking

3. Change your beliefs about stress.

Studies now show that simply changing your perception of stress from "being bad" to "being helpful" can improve your psychological well-being and lower mortality rates by 43%.

---

4. Stress in moderation helps build capacity to deal with life's inevitable happenings (like death, loss, heartbreak, being made redundant/laid off.)

5. Helping others can lower your mortality risk by 30%.

The brain fears the unknown. It likes to deal with reality, so if someone is too optimistic or too negative, it can be a stressor to the brain.

We all have a different capacity and tolerance for uncertainty.

Learning to accept how things are (even if you don't like it) and increasing your ability to label and name emotions can help you deal with your brain's reactions to the unknown. Reframing old mental models can help reduce amygdala activation and reactivity. (fight, flight or freeze responses).

> Getting sick is a major time thief and an emotional and energy drain, no matter how mild the virus, so taking care of your gut is critically important to creating a body and mind that thrive!

FOOD AND HEALTH

Your digestive system communicates with the brain primarily through the Vagus nerve, which runs from the brain stem to the gut. This communication is bidirectional, although the vast majority of the communication is from the gut to the brain.

The gut produces about 95% of the body's serotonin. Any abnormalities in the digestive system can directly shape both cognitive and emotional states.

A healthy diet may reduce anxiety, decrease the risk of depression and preserve cognitive functioning and brain volume into old age.

In one study, the difference in cognitive age between older adults eating a healthy diet and those eating an unhealthy one was 7.5 years.

You might ask what food is best for your brain and body?

The most studied diet that is beneficial is the Mediterranean diet which is rich in fruits and vegetables, olive oil, fish, lean meats, low sugar and processed foods.

Your gut health is also supported by healthy prebiotics such as (one of my favorites) *Kaibae™ Baobab Powder because of the company purpose and quality. Probiotics which come in a range of high-quality supplements or basic plain yogurt are key.

For those who use yogurt as their only probiotic, note that plain yogurt is best because flavored yogurts contain large quantities of sugar which can feed cancer, diabetes, obesity and bad bacteria in your gut. Just recently, I was looking at a small yogurt at a coffee shop in the United States and it had 10 teaspoons of sugar in a plain yogurt with fruit purée.

New scientific research indicates that your gut health impacts your immune system and mental wellbeing. It needs support to function effectively.

How much are you willing to invest in healthy quality probiotics and supplements?

Viome™.com is a company that I have used to do convenient in-home testing that you ship to their lab to determine what foods are your Superfoods and which foods you should minimize or avoid for optimal gut health and well-being.

They can also tell you which probiotics your gut needs to be at its best. They offer customized probiotics and personalized supplements based on your test results to increase your physical and mental performance.

Brain fog is a serious issue for many people. What you eat and drink dramatically impact the quality of your brain functions.

When I gave up foods that were not good for my brain and body, I experienced dramatic differences in my focus, my thoughts, feelings and ability to manage stressful situations.

I also eliminated my hot flashes by giving up sugar cane. This alone was worth the shift. More sleep, less sweating?

Sign me up!

I can still have chocolate made with honey and other natural sweeteners. Fortunately, there are plenty of delicious bars like HU to choose from and there is gelato without sugar cane in Italy where my heart said to go find it. (big smile!)

PHYSICAL ACTIVITY and EXERCISE

Just a modest amount of moderate intensity activity can take advantage of the brain's natural capacity for plasticity, improve cognition performance and academic achievement. It also reduces your risk of dementia.

Aerobic exercise preserves brain volume as you age and protects against other cognitive declines. I choose to walk every day to get groceries and carry the bags home to get my physical exercise as it's part of my integrated time saving, health practice. I don't like gyms, so nature is mine.

The brain remains plastic in old age.

Exercise increases a protein that supports the maintenance and growth of new neurons. It's called BDNF (brain-derived neurotrophic factor).

In younger people, including children, aerobic exercise can lead to improved memory performance and increased volume in the hippocampus in just a few weeks.

Note when training is stopped, hippocampal volume can decrease back to pre-training levels.

> Exercise is a level 1, Grade A Treatment for depression and can be effective for relieving anxiety.

DRINK WATER

1. Take care of your brain and body with plenty of water. Our bodies are at least 85% water and drinking plenty of water is essential for all systems to run optimally.

2. When you wake up in the morning you are dehydrated having not consumed water for 6-9 hours or more depending upon when you had your last glass of water.

3. Experiment with drinking at least 20 ounces of water upon waking.

    a. Many people report they no longer need coffee or caffeine to "get moving" in the morning after hydrating with plenty of water.

4. Depending upon where you live and how much you exercise, you may need more than the recommended 8 (16oz) glasses or 3 liters of fluids a day.

Remember that for every cup of caffeinated beverages you drink, your body needs an additional 1-2 cups of water to offset the dehydrating effects of the caffeine.

Studies show that peak performers sleep more (take naps to rest the brain), play more and do focused work about 4-5 hours a day.

SLEEP AND BRAIN HEALTH

1. Getting enough quality sleep at the right times can help protect your mental health, physical health, quality of life and safety.

2. Scientists say that most adults need 7 to 9 hours of sleep per night for optimal physical and mental performance.

3. Sleeping right after learning enhances your ability to retain information

4. Sleep improves performance in procedural skills.

5. Restricting sleep during the work week to be more productive is counter-productive.

6. Habitually not getting enough sleep (less than 7) reduces alertness, your ability to sustain attention to complete tasks, and your cognitive performance.

7. Sleep can't be "made up" in a weekend of normal sleep.

8. This can lead to micro sleeps which can have devastating effects.

Not Sleepy? Don't assume that because you're not sleepy, your level of alertness hasn't diminished. Humans are poor at judging how sleep deprived they are.

Other sleep hacks: Use a timer to turn off the wifi routers, no TV in the room, darken room or wear an eye shade to increase quality of sleep. Do not watch news before bed. Consider media fast to experiment with how it impacts you.

HEALTHY TIME SAVERS FOR YOUR BIOLOGY

Your body and brain need to move and keep your muscles strong. Try some of these time-saving body hacks.

Strengthen muscles while brushing your teeth: do squats, sit at the wall, calf raises or stretching.

Buy a stationary bicycle to put in your office and ride while you do your emailing or reading.

Strengthen arm muscles while driving (push arms into the steering wheel like a chest press).

Stand while riding the bus or working at a stand-up desk because sitting is the new smoking.

Walk to the store and carry groceries.

Take the stairs whenever possible.

Take a walk and catch up with people on the phone. Being in nature brings huge benefits for all parts of your body and mind. *Walking does not require the same brain functioning that more complicated work tasks require. (If you are walking in a city area, it's best not to walk and talk when there are multiple distractions and complicated dynamics that require attention to focus on for your safety).

SUMMARY

I invite you to experiment and practice some of these scientific based activities and behaviors the brain and body thrive on. Trust your experience and the results that you feel and see.

Remember: choose something small and easy to be done that enhances your work, health and focus first thing in your day so that you experience the dopamine hit the brain needs (reward). This sets up the Progress Loop that the brain loves. From this feeling and biochemical state, you set up the probability that your day will be much more productive.

DROP IT 2.0 PROCESS

Visioning
Awareness
Truth
Action

Visioning for Change

"If you can imagine it, you can become it." - *Einstein*

The first step to achieving any change is to envision the desired outcome. This works for individuals as well as organizations.

Take a moment to imagine a situation you're struggling with.

How would you like it to be instead of how it is?

Imagine as vividly as you can, the ideal state you desire.

See yourself taking the first courageous step to make this new desired state happen. Imagine you having the conversation, shifting your belief, doing just one small thing differently.

What will it feel like to have taken one step toward what you desire?

What impact and ripple effects will this have for you and your life, your organization imagining this change will happen?

Notice if you have any negative beliefs or stories running in this visioning process that could limit the possibilities for positive change. For now, just name them and acknowledge the desire to take a new action and bring your focus back toward your desired outcome/future state that you want for you and your organization. Let yourself imagine this fully.

Note how much time you'll save when the new change is in place.

IMPORTANT NEW SCIENTIFIC DATA TO NOTE ABOUT VISIONING AND VISUALIZATION

Scientists have continued studying visualization and have discovered that what we've been practicing around motivating ourselves using visualization and the principles taught in the "law of attraction" can be fine-tuned to be even more effective.

These new studies were focused on how visualization makes events seem real but, in fact, visualizing success is only wishful thinking. It substitutes the vision/fantasy of success for progress toward the goal of what you want to achieve.

Studies showed that fantasizing/visualizing a successful outcome caused a drop in energy leaving the person with less energy to work toward realizing the vision/fantasy.

It feels good to fantasize about celebrating our success before we achieve it. However, it's not enough.

This might be the explanation of why some people seem to manifest what they say they are visioning and those who don't.

Famous golfer, Jack Nicklaus, describes his visioning process for his golf game. In his words, "I use all 5 senses to make the shot. I imagine my feet on the grass, the smell of the fresh cut course, hearing the sounds of the wind or the leaves rustling nearby, feeling the body move through the perfect swing, hearing the club come in contact with the ball and feeling the vibration up my arms, watching the ball fly through the air and land exactly where I wanted it to land and finally the sensation of the short easy gentle stroke to get the ball into the cup. The best part is imagining the sound of the crowd clapping and bending over to pick the ball up out of the cup feeling the good sensations and joy."

THE STEPS TO SUCCESSFUL VISIONING

1. Create an expectation of success by mapping out your steps and visualize each and every one of the actions you need to take in order to achieve your desired outcome. Be very specific.

2. Feel all the sensations as if it is happening right now exactly as you want it to be.

3. Say out loud, "I choose this vision for myself."

It is helpful to visualize how you want your days to unfold, see yourself being present, accomplishing what you want and feeling your best.

Before presenting, use visioning to see yourself delivering exactly as you would ideally like to. Be specific about your feeling state, ability to speak concisely, receive questions and feedback gracefully.

Some people like to create vision boards with pictures and words that describe what they want to gain. Keep it somewhere you see regularly.

Celebrate successes!

Others like to write out their desired states and feelings to track their progress.

Others will do detailed project plans and set rewards for themselves when they achieve the results they desire.

Experiment with what works for you. Make it fun!

Visioning
Awareness
Truth
Action

Whatever it is that drains your energy,

holds you hostage to the past,

runs over and over through your mind,

makes you sick and tired

or creates guilt and self punishment

is what you want to discover and name.

You can tame it by calculating the costs

and telling the truth

so that you can exercise your will

to choose freedom and

learn to Drop It.

This is a process that will enhance your

effectiveness, presence, health and

relationship with yourself and others.

> *You can't outrun what runs inside you.*

Holding it All Together

Fear of Failure

Self Criticism

The Need to Be Right

It's Never Enough

Complaining

Worry and Dread

I Am Not Good Enough

Lack of Motivation

I'm Too Old to Change

Refusing to Accept the Truth

I Don't Belong Here

Old hurts, pain and sadness

Closed Minded, Rigid, Chaotic

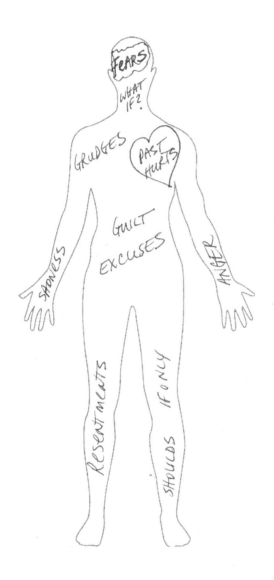

How present can you be with this inside?

What else is running inside you?

and

How much time and energy are spent when that is running?

What is it costing you? And your team?

 *negative self-talk*

 worrying about what might happen in the future

 guilt for not doing what I say I want to do

fear of not getting it right

replaying conversations

believing that things won't change

Other things that run inside and steal your time and freedom

_____

_____

What STORIES and NEGATIVE BELIEFS run inside you?

I'm too ...

It's not possible...

I don't...

I am not ...

I can't ...

They will never...

Stories and negative beliefs are powerful constructs we hold as truth. We come to expect and have experiences that confirm these long-held beliefs.

It is said, "You get what you expect."

These stories and beliefs become a prison in your mind that you are held hostage by. They can run and ruin your health, relationships and life.

 One of my old stories was:

UNLESS IT'S HARD OR DIFFICULT, IT'S NOT WORTH DOING

This cost me huge amounts of time and energy over-working and unnecessary stress that limited my presence. Things that came easily were shunned as less than worthy ventures.

Fortunately, that old story is no longer robbing me of time and mind space. I finally used these tools to identify what was truly running inside me and recognized what it was costing me and my life. The truth helped me see the reality so I could make a conscious choice to Drop It.

Over the years, I've seen very unique and unusual stories and beliefs based on culture, geographics, and social demographics. And then there are the universal ones.

One of the universal stories I often hear is what I call the NEVERLAND DESTINATION RESORT OR RUT that people take up occupancy in and stay for far too long.

This one major internal program can consume all possibilities of something different ever happening in a person's life.

Take note of all the stories you tell yourself that begin with:

I WILL NEVER...

I will never...

_____

_____

_____

_____

_____

How much time and mind space do these consume?

What will be possible when I move out of my NEVERLAND DESTINATION RUT?

A tool is only useful if I actually use it.

Take a moment to acknowledge other tools you've learned and used in your life before now to help you to grow and change.

Let's dig into this new Drop It Tool more now!

DROP IT 2.0 Process

1. VISIONING to Clarify My Desired Outcome

What's right for right now?

2. AWARENESS of What is Running Inside Me?

What are the costs?

3. TELL THE TRUTH – Discover/Gather Evidence

For the sake of WHAT am I going to *Drop It*?

4. Take ACTION to Empty Out

Everything that happens begins with a conversation either with yourself or another.

Coaching is a conversation with yourself or another that supports targeted change and development.

Often times a coaching engagement is precipitated by a "call to action" by the individual or their organization. When a coach works with a client, they start by exploring what it is that the client aspires to create instead of what is happening now.

Coaching is a conversation that supports targeted change. You can become your own best coach by applying the same process with yourself. You have conversations with yourself all day long. From the minute you wake up and ask yourself, "Will I hit the snooze button or get up now?"

This tool teaches you to shift your inner conversations for good.

Human beings in general are less likely to implement the changes they say they want to make unless there is immediacy. This means that you don't seek to change until you need to.

> We are more motivated to take action to rectify the suffering we are experiencing when our pain threshold has been exceeded.

Which means we really won't change until it hurts too much NOT to change. This is a strange reality that we experience in ourselves and we also observe in others.

People act when they recognize that what they are doing is costing them more than they truly can afford. The physical, mental, financial or emotional costs become so high that it creates the impulse that propels them to take action.

Or not.

Sometimes they do not take action and the costs continue to rise and more losses ensue. For some it's their health or their very life. For others it's their next missed opportunity, failure to perform to expectations, divorce or other wake-up call that forces the issue into "I HAVE TO change now."

Awareness of the pain and what it is costing you is key to evoking action to create a new possible desired outcome.

You must take a journey that helps you identify and become more aware of the things that are depleting your energy and getting in the way of you being more present and productive.

If you are currently in the "I want/need to" or "I have to" stage of the desire to change, this tool is designed to walk you through the process of evaluating what you might **DROP** in order to create sustainability and new possibilities for you, your organization, your team, your family and your life.

One of the steps to creating lasting change and increasing your productivity, presence and possibilities is to assess where you are hurting and determine if the pain is pressing enough to take action steps right now.

You now have the opportunity to reflect and write as you journey through the many varieties of physical, mental, emotional and financial energy leaks that are draining you and reducing your productivity, presence and freedom.

Today's environment requires enormous energy reserves to deal with the demanding work lives we each have. The work week has been extended. You likely have hundreds of emails to respond to in any given day or week. The expectations continue to increase around how you "show up" and authentically engage with your workforce and your loved ones.

Leaders face the on-going pressure to be great managers and continually inspire others to give their best in the organizations they work for. Their ability to bring positive vitality and a happy presence does impact an organization's productivity.

How does a leader learn to exert and sustain the tremendous amount of positive energy and presence now required?

First, it's important to analyze where resources are allocated.

You will now look at where you SPEND your physical and mental energy in any given day, week, month or year, then assess how much time you spend thinking about the past, reliving old experiences, replaying mistakes, or focusing on lost opportunities.

Key explorations will then ensue regarding what is "eating away at you" and draining your inner psychological and emotional resources.

Other key energy leaks including old stories in your head, outdated negative beliefs, should(s), self-criticism, judgments, dread, resentments, grudges, regrets, debilitating dialogues, denial of the truth and self-sabotage, can then be considered.

Significant energy loss occurs when you are plagued with DISTRACTIONS, SELF SABOTAGE, INACTION and EXCUSES.

This sets up GUILT CYCLES that drain you even more.

Change always requires ACTION.

I am inviting you to embark on a new way to increase your productivity, presence and freedom by learning to *Drop It* and *Empty Out* that which no longer serves you right now and experience new possibilities beyond your current imagination.

You can bring more clearly into view that which is debilitating your capacity to gain 20/20 vision into what you want now in your life. This first step will require a commitment to give an old cliché a fair chance at supporting you in ways you might not have imagined:

The truth will set you free,

And it will likely piss you off or hurt at first.

In my experience, the truth always sets me free and it often is painful to see how I am my own worst enemy. I get in my own way often.

Let's start to bring things into 20/20 focus by exploring an assortment of truths for you to reflect and write about as you dive into the heart of the inner work.

When you can name, discover and accept what is true in this moment, you can begin to see what can be changed and what can be done about the past that can't be changed.

I invite you to be courageous in this moment and tell yourself the deep truth that needs to be unearthed to gain your freedom. Note that it is ok to name a desired truth, even if you have no plans to act upon it at this time.

Dreaming is an exploration. It is not a place for hesitation.

Sometimes we want something and yet we can't have it right now. I invite you to let yourself have the freedom to explore what is living deep inside you. Be bold and don't hold back.

<u>What are you aware of that you want most at this time in your life?</u>

Personally?

Professionally?

I say one thing
and
I do another.

Truth #1

I say one thing and I do another.

Reflect and write about all the things you say you want but are doing something else:

Mistakes refine me. They do not define me.

Mistakes refine me. They do not define me.

Reflect and write about any of the ways you have defined yourself by mistakes you've made in the past or are still carrying within yourself as old pain or heaviness:

I have blamed others for my situation.

I have blamed others for my situation.

Reflect and write about who or what you have blamed:

I can't save others who don't want help.

I can't save others who don't want help.

Reflect and write about how hard you've worked at rescuing:

I am carrying past hurts.

I am carrying past hurts.

Reflect and write about how you feel about this and what you are carrying from the past that you want to let go of:

I am not fully present with people I care about.

I am not fully present with people I care about.

Reflect and write about what this is costing you and them:

I have to take action to change.

Truth #7

I have to take action to change.

Reflect and write about what gets in the way of you using your power to shift and take steps to create what you want:

I create
the guilt
that I feel.

I create the guilt that I feel.

Reflect and write about what you are mad at yourself for:

I am faking it
and
going through
the motions.

Truth #9

I am faking it and going through the motions.

Reflect and write about how you are pretending, incongruent, inauthentic or out of integrity in your life and relationships:

I only have

one

precious

life.

HARNESS TIME and FREE YOUR MIND

I only have one precious life.

Reflect and write about how you are not living this truth:

I judge myself and others.

HARNESS TIME and FREE YOUR MIND

I judge myself and others.

Reflect and write upon what the costs are to you and others:

I betray myself.

Truth #12

I betray myself.

Reflect and write about how you betray yourself and deny your own health and happiness:

I "should" on myself and others.

I "should" on myself and others.

Reflect and write about the "shoulds" you use:

I allow negative thinking and fears to steal my time and energy.

I allow negative thinking and fear to steal my energy and time.

Reflect and write about who you learned this from and what gets in the way of you shifting your negative thoughts and feelings:

My excuses are excessive and expensive.

My excuses are excessive and expensive

List the excuses you use most and what they are costing you:

I get stuck in victim thinking.

I get stuck in victim thinking.

Reflect and write about how and where you are playing the victim and feel powerless to create something else?

Busy-ness
is tyranny
to my heart.

Busy-ness is tyranny to my heart.

Reflect and write about your busy-ness and the costs to you and others you love and care about:

I invalidate myself and others.

I invalidate myself and others.

Reflect on this and write about what you would like instead:

Staying stuck
is a choice.

Staying stuck is a choice.

Reflect and write about where you are choosing to stay stuck:

I Am
The
Decisive
Element.

I Am the Decisive Element

I have come to the frightening conclusion that I am the decisive element. It is my personal approach that creates tremendous power to make life miserable or joyous. I can be a tool of torture or an instrument of inspiration; I can humiliate or humor, hurt or heal. In all situations, it is my response that decides whether a crisis is escalated or de-escalated, and a person humanized or de-humanized.

Johann Wolfgang von Goethe

Reflect upon your personal approach and how you want to respond instead of react going forward:

> You may or may not be surprised by anything you read or discover about yourself now.

However, you may be surprised by how much it can change your life quickly if you allow yourself to see, accept and ACT UPON THE TRUTH of your current reality and take action to CHANGE the things that do not serve you any longer.

You can harness time and free your mind.

You can create the clear 20/20 vision of how you want to be present and free of all the unconscious saboteurs in order to have a more productive, healthy and authentic life right now.

If you apply your free will and use the tools to drop those things that sabotage you, you can gain more of what you want in your life personally and professionally.

Change can happen more quickly than you think when you use tools that work with your biology and 3 brains.

Awareness is the first step to change.

AWARENESS is the first step to change.

You now will have an opportunity to use your keen senses, engage your curiosity and build your capacity to observe yourself and practice taking note of what is actually happening in your day-to-day life. We call them blind spots.

It is more TRUTH TELLING.

You may be surprised at first, but the clarity will be worth the effort and it will likely help spur you to an action that will support you in getting what you truly want.

In the following pages you will find a list of things that can consume a significant amount of your time in any given day.

Sometimes activities we engage in are not called distractions as they have a higher perceived value such as watching the news, exercising, socializing.

In this following exercise you are looking at time allocated for various activities. The things on this list may be the very activities that repeatedly distract you from accomplishing the things you want to do and living the life you want now.

Some of these activites are likely harming your relationships as your presence is required to connect, communicate and collaborate at work and at home.

Your presence directly impacts the quality of engagement with yourself and with others.

What are you spending your time and presence doing?

Let's take a look at where you are allocating your time, your thoughts, precious resources and energy.

I am engaged in the following:

Activity	How much time per day
☐ Ineffective meetings	_____
☐ Thinking about the past	_____
☐ Day dreaming/future	_____
☐ Reliving conversations	_____
☐ Talking about others	_____
☐ Worrying	_____
☐ Exercising	_____
☐ Cleaning/puttering	_____
☐ Complaining about work	_____
☐ Negative self talk	_____
☐ Retelling stories	_____
☐ Family drama	_____
☐ Internet search	_____
☐ Social media	_____
☐ On-line dating	_____
☐ Television	_____
☐ Video games	_____
☐ Shopping therapy	_____
☐ Junk email	_____
☐ Reading magazines	_____
☐ Smoking	_____
☐ Eating/Drinking	_____
☐ _____	_____

What strikes me most about the total time I spend engaging in these various activities?

How do these activities really affect my productivity, presence, health and well-being?

What impact are they having on my relationship with myself and others?

How open, curious and available am I?

THE COSTS OF DISTRACTION

What are the real costs of my energy leaks? To me and others around me?

What will be possible when I drop some of these activities and regain more of my focused presence and quality time?

The Power of Presence
And Cost of Technological Distractions

An informal experiment was done on the negative impact of cell phones and perceived quality time spent around them.

The team each had their daily one-on-one brief morning check-in which was scheduled routinely for 10 minutes each.

The boss had their cell phone on the desk while meeting with each separately. (It didn't ring, they didn't look at it. It was just visible on the desk during the time spent with the employee).

When they came out after 10 minutes, they were asked how long did your boss spend with you? They all said 3 minutes.

The next week, the boss put the phone in a drawer so it wasn't visible during the 10-minute check ins.

When they came out after 10 minutes, they reported that they spent 30 minutes.

*When asked after what caused the huge discrepancy between their perceived time together. Each reported various comments about even though their boss didn't answer the phone, they were perceiving that they must be expecting an important call, so hurry up with your update.

Versus when there was no phone visible, they were not distracted by the device and were more present themselves.

Self Sabotage

Reflect and check the boxes for how I sabotage myself:

- ☐ Resist change/stay the same
- ☐ Put too many things on my list that I can't complete
- ☐ Drink too much alcohol and feel terrible the next day
- ☐ Eat foods that I know I shouldn't eat and then beat myself up about it afterwards
- ☐ Ignore my inner voice, intuition and my gut feelings
- ☐ Expect too much of myself and how I should behave
- ☐ Negative self-talk/Self doubt
- ☐ Hyper critical of everything I say and do
- ☐ False promises to myself and others
- ☐ Low expectations of myself/too high of expectations
- ☐ Relive mistakes and hold them over my own head
- ☐ Beat myself up about what I'm doing or not doing
- ☐ Set unrealistic goals
- ☐ Ignore my physical and emotional needs
- ☐ Don't get enough sleep
- ☐ I should fix others issues for them
- ☐ Don't see a doctor when I need to
- ☐ Take drugs to distract/numb out
- ☐ Drink too much coffee/soda/energy drinks
- ☐ Don't let myself have any fun
- ☐ Resist doing what's best for me
- ☐ Deprive myself of what I truly want

- ☐ Give up on my dreams, hopes and wishes
- ☐ Watch TV instead of living life/having adventures
- ☐ Tell myself I'm happy when I'm not
- ☐ Lie awake recounting all the things I didn't do right or didn't finish instead of focusing on what I did well
- ☐ Invalidating myself and my value in work and life
- ☐ Living in the past
- ☐ Lying to myself and others
- ☐ Addicted to drama/chaos
- ☐ Choosing suffering over freedom and relief
- ☐ Allowing fear to stop me from taking action
- ☐ Betraying my integrity/values
- ☐ Settling for less than I deserve or want
- ☐ Ignoring warning signs
- ☐ Pretending/being inauthentic
- ☐ Not speaking my truth
- ☐ Martyrdom
- ☐ Over responsibility for everyone and everything
- ☐ Can't relax and have fun
- ☐ This is how I've always done it
- ☐ This is what my parents did
- ☐ "Yes, but not now"
- ☐ "How dare you want so much"
- ☐ "It won't work"
- ☐ "I can't"

Estimate how much time and energy you engage in these self-sabotaging conversations with yourself.

What is this costing you?

What will be possible when you stop harassing yourself?

Let's talk about the last one on the self-sabotaging list.

I CAN'T.

Humans often tell themselves that the gap between knowledge and action is bigger than it really is.

Remember we're working to not believe a lot of what we think since most of it is negative.

The truth is.

When you say I CAN, YOU CAN!

And if you say the opposite, "I can't" then you won't be able to.

Remember a time when you told yourself, "I CAN" and you could.

Where in your life do you need to be dropping the "I CAN'T" and start saying "I CAN" more?

Working with HOW our brains work is how we create change.

Experiment and trust your own experience of this.

Change your behavior you change your brain. Remember your brain is built on past experiences.

Visioning
is a Tool
for Change and
Action
Planning

Let's imagine that you CAN and you WILL harness time and free your mind. You have free will choice to take action or not.

The brain does not distinguish between imagining and actually doing an action. Athletes have practiced their sport and every detailed action step involved in their training, preparation, performing and the outcome of victory, thousands of times in their minds before competitions.

Remember the head brain's objective is to accurately predict the future. Therefore, each time you visualize the steps and the outcomes you desire and feel, hear, sense and taste the entire process to get the victory, you are building a new brain.

Change your brain, change your behavior.

Neuroscientists have confirmed in studies recently that people who only do "fantasizing and visualization" of the outcome have a drop in energy and often lose motivation to take the actual steps necessary to get what they hope to achieve.

The brain needs specific steps and details that include feeling states to simulate what you want to achieve.

Visioning also allows you the opportunity to experiment and imagine doing something you've never done before and experience the new outcome as if it has already happened. This opens you to the possibilities of creating behavior change and results.

Often times when you are learning to do something differently in your life, you will bump up against resistance.

Sometimes your resistance comes from not knowing what it will be like on the other side of the action step you want or need to take. Sometimes it's from the fear of change.

One way you can begin to explore what might be possible is to pretend, imagine and envision yourself using **Drop It** first.

This gives you an opportunity to practice using the power of your mind to perform the steps necessary and experiencing the steps and actions with no risk. This can increase your probability of making your vision a reality in the future.

> *People imagine and envision differently.*
> *Some people see things visually,*
> *Others may hear more and some smell, taste or*
> *feel things while they are imagining.*

Whatever you experience is what is right for you.

Notice if any internal dialogue comes up for you when you try something new or different. Try to resist any self-sabotaging thoughts you may start having right now like "I can't visualize" or "This won't work for me."

Acknowledge anything that could get in the way of you trying this.

And then choose to **DROP IT**.

A VISION PRACTICE OF DROP IT

I invite you now to experience a somatic exercise in which you will envision and imagine what might be possible for you if these stories, beliefs, activities, distractions and self-sabotaging behaviors you have identified so far were not plaguing you.

It is a short vision that takes you through the steps to **Drop It**.

I used the word plague above because it's quite possible that when you close your eyes and let your body sense what all these self-sabotaging behaviors feel like, look like and smell like, it might be plague-like and the energy may feel like a heavy object that occupies a lot of space within you.

If you're ready to release all that and free your mind, let's begin.

<u>First</u>:

Read through your checklists of distractions and self-harassment and notice the energy each one of these behaviors carries. Begin to feel that energy.

1. Now close your eyes and visualize yourself reading this book and answering the questions to gain clarity on what you are now aware of. Feel in your body what the truth telling revealed. Bring to mind an image of the totality of your checklists and sense the size, shape and color as well as the feelings and sensations you experience as you mingle with these activities and self-sabotaging behaviors.

2. Once you have a sense of this, connect with your desire to be free of this negative energy system draining you.

3. Imagine taking all of these distractions, self-sabotaging behaviors, thoughts and beliefs out of you and see them outside your body now.

4. You are holding the energy system in your hands.

5. Now imagine or sense a large body of calm water before you and connect with your desire to let go of these saboteurs. Feel how much you want to be free.

6. **Drop It** into the water as you make a conscious choice to take action to LET IT ALL GO.

7. Imagine that you have dropped the negative energy into a lake or large pool of water and as it hits you watch as the ripples expand outward.

8. Take a deep breath.

9. Feel the relief and freedom having released it. Take another deep breath.

10. Now imagine having more time and a free mind to be present, connected and productive.

11. Say outload, "I choose this vision for myself."

What sensations do you feel now having envisioned Dropping It?

What will be possible when you feel more of these sensations running inside you instead?

How will these positive feelings impact your productivity and your team's productivity?

Did you know that research says that an employee's productivity and engagement is directly related to the MOOD OF THEIR BOSS?

Imagine the impact this new positive energy will bring you and others.

For The Sake Of What Am I Willing To Drop More?

For the sake of my...

freedom

health and wellness

peace of mind

job effectiveness

getting what I've always wanted

joy and happiness

energy and vitality

space and time

opportunity for different outcomes

a good night's sleep

my relationships with family/children

creating a positive legacy

success at work and in my relationships

leadership effectiveness and retention

ease and flow

relief

balance

fresh start/new beginning

doing what makes sense to me now

clarity, wisdom and action that leads to better results

Dreaded Drama and DisEase

I took a course from David Emerald and Donna Zajonc who wrote the book, *TED The Empowerment Dynamic,* which taught me about the Dreaded Drama Triangle or DDT for short.

Simply put, this triangle is made up of 3 ways of being: the Victim, the Rescuer and the Perpetrator. When you and others are engaged in being in any one of these positions on the DDT there is drama. And you, can do all 3 to yourself and spend a lot of your precious time in any and all of these for hours, days, weeks or years.

This dynamic is happening all around us at home and at work.

Take note of how you play the victim at times:

What are the costs of rescuing for you and others?

Where are you perpetrating and hurting yourself or others?

Drama is everywhere and it can be transformed when you become aware that you are engaged in it and recognize that you are being hurt by it and acknowledge the costs of staying stuck in it.

The opportunity to free yourself from this massive time and energy draining vortex is to choose to take action and use your *Drop It* tools and *Empty Out* so you can shift from:

Victim to **Creator**

Rescuer to **Coach**

Perpetrator to **Challenger**

Ghosts Grudges and Guilt

A Poison Tree

I was angry with my friend;
I told my wrath, my wrath did end.

I was angry with my foe:
I told it not, my wrath did grow.

- William Blake

Resentments, grudge-carrying and harboring old hurts deplete us and create drama and dis-ease. It's all the things that eat away at us that harm our work and lives. This limits our ability to be present.

Our bodies and minds become mired in what I call self-induced suffering. We do have free will choice to carry or Drop anything.

I invite you to experience new levels of relief in this experience and practice of emptying out to find new freedom of mind:

1. Bring to mind a grudge, old hurt, betrayal or resentment you have carried.

2. Name the person who hurt you.

3. When did this happen?

4. So how long have you carried it?

5. If you imagine this resentment has a shape, color and energy to it where does it reside inside your body?

6. What do you notice is happening inside you as you bring this energy into your awareness now?

What amount of emotional and physical energy is activated when you relive this hurt or resentment that you've held inside yourself?

What is it really costing YOU to hang on to this?

What would be possible if you could *EMPTY OUT* and *DROP IT*?

Notice and write about any resistances you're experiencing right now in considering this ACTION:

Resistance is normal and carrying the past is also something we often do because our family of origin likely taught us to suffer and create more drama by hanging on to things.

Sometimes we believe that if we hold on to it then they can't hurt us again. But like the Poison Tree poem William Blake wrote, if you hold on to it, you suffer more.

What are you afraid might happen if you *DROP IT*?

What if you resisted your resistance and just imagined for a moment that you reached into your body and pulled the resentment, hurt or grudge out of you and let yourself *DROP IT*?

Breathe deeply.

Envision doing that.

Notice what you feel as you imagine dropping it and name the sensations.

EMPTY OUT

DROP IT 2.0

I have discovered a new combination of emptying out that has become a game changing addition to the *Drop It* methodology. It is a two-step process which is powerfully effective in dealing with past hurts, betrayals, grudges, guilt, missteps, breaches, resentments and any events that have caused you pain, frustration, resentment or others you love and care about.

Emotions are energy. They are messengers to alert us as to our physical and emotional state of our nervous system and body. We have hundreds of emotions running within us. Many we are not conscious of and sometimes we have more than one at a time. For example, fear and excitement can feel the same and sometimes we may have both at the same time when doing something new, or going somewhere we've never been.

Before we begin the empty out process. Let me clarify what anger is, because my experience is that many people are uncomfortable with this emotion. Or others in your life have not allowed you to name and express it in healthy ways.

Anger is a messenger that tells us that what is happening/or happened is NOT OK.

Anger is about boundary setting.

Where do you need to say NO more?

When we have a clear NO, we also have a clear YES.

Anger is a very useful feeling because it provides important information for us to listen to and utilize in a safe and effective manner.

There are healthy and safe ways to express anger and release to free your body and mind of past hurts.

Often times beneath anger is hurt and sadness.

We are now going to experience and learn the steps to **Empty Out** the anger, hurt and sadness you're carrying energetically.

THE EMPTY OUT PROCESS

1. Write an anger letter to the person who hurt you.

    a. Use the feeling language and words you're not supposed to ever say to another, and express exactly the sensations of pain, suffering, anger, rage and disgust.

    b. Write quickly and let the anger fuel the process.

    c. Keep writing until you are emptied out and have nothing more to say.

    d. If you wrote it on paper, please burn it

    e. If you typed it on a computer, please delete it

    f. Once you've emptied out, go out in nature if possible and breathe deeply and feel the sensations you have within having written and expressed your anger and hurt at this situation or person who hurt you.

*If you start feeling more anger and need to say more, go back and use the fuel of the moment to keep writing. This emptying out may take you to other hurts you have had in your life.

2. Write the apology letter you deserve that you are never going to get.

    a. Say exactly what you would want this other person to say to you in a thorough apology letter, leaving nothing out.

    b. Read it out loud to yourself. Feel the words land within.

    c. Take a few deep breaths and read it again. Keep reading or writing what you want and need to hear to find the freedom and feeling state you want.

    d. You can save these or release them through burning.

This is a tool for life to keep yourself "emptied out" of anything that steals your energy, freedom, vitality, focus and ability to be more present to the here and now. Choose to *Empty Out* as soon as something happens to stay free and present always.

Grudges We Hold Against Ourselves

Now bring to mind a time that you got hurt because YOU did not protect yourself.

Name the time, place and event details of this experience:

How long have you carried this against yourself?

Reflect on how much energy is expended to carry what you hold against yourself inside your body and mind:

If you imagine this resentment has a shape, color and energy to it, where does it reside inside your body?

What happens to your emotional and mental energy when you relive this specific hurt or resentment you hold toward yourself?

What is it costing YOU to relive and hang onto this?

How might this be keeping you from being more fully present?

What will be possible when you **DROP THIS** and **EMPTY OUT**?

REPETITIVE

DEBILITATING

DIALOGUES

With Self

And

Others

What are the repetitive dialogues you have with yourself that you wish would stop?

What are the repetitive dialogues you have with others that you wish would stop?

How much time do you spend talking about others to others?

What is the quality of the energy within yourself when you are talking about others in this way?

What conversations do you have with yourself before bed at night?

What do you say to yourself when you look in a mirror?

What do you do to distract yourself or numb out from your pain, stress, overwhelm or negative judgments and repetitive conversations you have with yourself?

(i.e. drink, watch TV, internet, shop, eat, work more, avoid others)

How are these limiting your presence, capacity to focus, perform and model a healthy lifestyle for others at work and at home?

What would be possible if you could have different conversations with yourself and others?

Imagine it exactly as you would like it to be?

What's one thing you could do differently that you've never tried before to stop these repetitive conversations?

What belief (about yourself or the other) would you have to let go of, in order to create the outcomes you imagine and desire?

Visualize yourself using your Drop It and Empty Out tools to clear whatever needs to be cleared to take ACTION to change. See yourself taking the small steps to do what needs to be done.

Imagine the entire process step by step and feel what it will feel like when you are having productive, validating, and empowering conversations with yourself and others.

May you find ease in being self-validating of your growth each step of the way. Be bold and don't wait to take small steps now.

The change and transformation journey requires courage, compassion and empathy for self and others as well as EFFORT.

You can create new behaviors and change your brain no matter how old you are. One shift at a time.

> Through repetition and effort, the brain and body learn to shape itself around new positive habits, thoughts, feelings and experiences you engage in.

I hope that you will claim your power and go take action to build a more positive, healthy, vibrant and peaceful brain and body by what you will do, say, think, eat and feel to support your well-being.

I hope that you will choose to be encouraging to yourself and others as you journey through life continuing to learn new habits and grow.

I hope that you will build a new habit of Dropping It and Emptying Out so you can enjoy the one precious life you have with more time, peace, presence and possibility.

I hope that you won't wait to use this tool regularly in your life.

It all comes down to what you are willing to do to change.

Notice if you are afraid to change. Who taught you this from the past? What does your fear keep you from having?

When it's all said and done. You shape yourself and your life by what you do, say, think and feel.

If you want more time, energy and presence, you CAN have it.

"When you empty out, the murky waters will clear and ripples will move out to form a new energy field and spaciousness that harnesses time and frees your mind. Here is where your presence, focus, inspiration, creativity, resilience and productivity can expand and thrive."

-Linda Newlin

Drop It
In Action:
Inspiring
Change

INSPIRING CHANGE

In an attempt to inspire you to continue to drop anything that no longer serves you, I've listed the following things that clients have taken ACTION on and found more productivity, presence, freedom and possibility in their lives.

Examples of things people Drop:

☐ Waiting for commitment/marriage

☐ Passed over for promotion

☐ Raise/bonus not as high as expected

☐ Having to train someone promoted over me

☐ Not getting the relocation assignment I requested

☐ Made redundant/downsized/fired

☐ Bankruptcy/losing money in investments

☐ Broken heart/engagement called off

☐ Divorce/Affairs

☐ Disppointments

☐ Being used

☐ Misled for a Green Card/Immigration to country

☐ Loss of money from stock market crash

☐ Infertility

☐ Cancer Survivor (as an identity)

☐ Money loaned and not returned

☐ Left by a partner for same sex relationship

- ☐ Unrealistic expectations of addicted family members
- ☐ Not finishing college
- ☐ The love that got away
- ☐ Not making the pro team
- ☐ Not leaving a small town to explore the world
- ☐ Not being able to stop a loved one from suicide
- ☐ Survivor guilt
- ☐ Causing accidents that harmed others
- ☐ Failing bar exam
- ☐ Thrown under the bus by someone
- ☐ Unsupported by boss or family members
- ☐ Given up for adoption
- ☐ Resentment over a sibling who was a favorite
- ☐ Performance Review that felt inaccurate and unfair
- ☐ Dreams that went unfulfilled
- ☐ Not graduating with honors
- ☐ Company won't pay for my advanced degree
- ☐ Going into a career my parents wanted
- ☐ Settling
- ☐ Loved ones who died serving others in the line of duty
- ☐ Resentments held against parents
- ☐ Blaming self for abuse suffered at the hands of others

- ☐ Not seeking medical treatment soon enough
- ☐ Loss of a loved one and not moving on to love again
- ☐ I could have...
- ☐ I should have...
- ☐ If only ... I would have...
- ☐ Unrealistic expectations of self and others
- ☐ DUI/Past crimes
- ☐ Others not liking me
- ☐ Complaining
- ☐ Hoping for something but taking no action to get it
- ☐ Telling myself I have no choice or "I have to"
- ☐ "I don't have time to work out" making excuses daily
- ☐ If only they would...
- ☐ Quitting smoking is too hard
- ☐ I'll try/I've tried
- ☐ Projects left incomplete
- ☐ New Year's resolutions not fulfilled
- ☐ Comparing myself to others
- ☐ Fear of failure
- ☐ Fear of success
- ☐ Afraid to die/Afraid to live/Afraid to love
- ☐ Afraid to take risks

Here are some inspiring ways clients have used these tools. I've included the steps they took for you to see the process from Coaching for Change, Awareness, Truth Telling and Action!

The results were beyond just harnessing time and freeing their mind. Remember, one small shift leads to big changes over time and change can happen quickly.

These are just a few examples to encourage you to experiment with new information, new thinking and keep a beginner's exploratory mindset in your journey and change process.

Validation of Changes

Job/Life Satisfaction

Writing a Book

Healthy Weight

Free From Legal Battle

Owning The Calendar

VALIDATION OF CHANGE

My client was working to increase his ability to delegate and develop his team. He needed to elevate his leadership to the next level and stop being IN the business, but be more ON the business. He first used the Empty Out tools to drop the past reactions around feedback he received that was a surprise.

He identified old patterns and unconscious beliefs that were keeping him from letting go and getting out of the weeds. He was using the Drop It Tools as he committed to removing any obstacles that were getting in his way of achieving the desired outcome. He made a significant change in his personal life as he courageously told the truth to himself that his relationship was not healthy and moving out of the dynamic was the right thing for him and his family. He stopped drinking alcohol as it impacted his presence, sleep, focus and mood.

He was thriving and his vision of having more flow was working. His behavior and brain have changed. He is able to be present and more concise in his communications with the CEO and MTeam. He thinks different thoughts and eats differently.

He is developing his leadership team by delegating more. He recently went away for an entire week and unplugged for the first time ever. He normally has 1500 emails, but he came back to only a few hundred (which were mostly informs).

I validated him and pointed out how incredible his growth has been in a short amount of time. He discovered in that moment that he was programed in childhood to not invalidate growth in himself and others. I recommended a Validation Practice!

Change is possible in a short amount of time.

You can create what you want if you take different actions.

JOB/LIFE SATISFACTION

My client was upset that he'd been passed over for several recent job openings at his company. He came for coaching.

In the Awareness process he discovered that one of his priorities for the next six years is spending time with his teen boys and his wife as they prepare for an empty nest.

The Truth is that his current management role allows him to work a flexible time schedule so he can be home for his son's games or practices in the late afternoons if he starts before 7 a.m. This schedule also allows him to miss the heavy morning traffic and rush hour traffic. He makes great money with retirement benefits and gets tons of vacation time.

He also identified that he had some special projects he could take on to keep his "interest" and fulfillment going over the next several years in his current leadership role.

After working through the **Drop It** Process he could let go of his resentment for being "passed over" for new opportunities and focus on what he really wants now. His current role does fulfill his love of developing his staff, building customer relationships "and" it allows him to be the father and husband he wants to be during the next six years.

Being passed over for new opportunities at work.

The truth set him free to see, he has what he wants right now.

WRITING A BOOK

I have worked with many clients who have wanted to write a book. Each of them have had to *DROP* things in order to actually write one.

All of these will sound very rational and are a clear articulation of why the resistance is grounded in the stance of "I can't write a book." See if any of these apply to you in any way around other things in your life you are resisting and/or saying "I can't."

- ❒ "I can't until I have enough experience to be credible."

- ❒ "I don't want to produce anything if it isn't perfect."

- ❒ "I can write an article easily, but don't think I could write an entire book."

- ❒ "I want to write something original, but there is no original thought left."

- ❒ "What if no one buys it?"

- ❒ "If I can't write a best seller, then I don't want to write anything."

- ❒ "No one wants to hear my story."

- ❒ "I don't think of myself as a writer."

- ❒ "I'm afraid of being rejected by publisher's."

- ❒ "I want to have control over the book and publisher's don't let you."

- ❒ "I don't know what I would call the book."

- ❒ "It takes a really long time to write a book."

All valid points.

Any one of these could keep you from ever writing a book for sure. However, if you want to write a book then choosing to **Drop** your particular roadblocks to doing what you say you want to do is the secret.

Remember the **Drop It** Process.

The first step is identifying what you want and what's holding you back from taking action to have it.

AWARENESS

Shine light on the limitations and beliefs held.

TELL THE TRUTH

It is in the discovering and uncovering of truth that helps you consider another perspective and potential new information as it relates to your long standing roadblocks that have detoured you from accomplishing things you say you want to do.

In this particular arena of writing a book my client discovered many enlightening things by seeking new truths while she talked with other authors and researched what is true about many "best selling" authors in her desired area of focus.

TRUTH #1

Authors are not always experts in a topic they write about.

She discovered that often it is people who have experienced valuable insights in their work and life's journey that decided to share it with the world. Depending on what you are wanting to write about, your level of expertise and time in a profession may have nothing to do with your credibility to write. It has more to do with your authentic experience and ability to tell the story of what you want to share.

Another client wanted to write about DEFINING MOMENTS based on her own experience of leaving a very successful career at the largest multinational software company and moving into an international coaching practice that she created. She also wanted to share the stories of her clients (confidentially) of how they have navigated the defining moments in their lives.

When we walked through her long list of "resistances" and self-inflicted objections to overcome, it became clear that she could **TAKE ACTION** and **DROP** a number of things quite easily upon accessing the **TRUTH.** These truths included:

1. She could self-publish and have control over the content, cover design, distribution and profit more from sales than using a publisher.

2. She connected to the "purpose" of what she wanted the book to do for others in sharing her story and the stories of others. She wanted to INSPIRE people.

3. She found the title to her book by talking through the "for the sake of 'what' do I want to write this book."

4. She reflected on how easy it is for her to write articles and recognized that the length of her desired book was the total of all she had already written to date.

5. She envisioned how this could help people in the world and her desire to act sooner rather than later was activated.

6. She asked her clients if they would share their stories for her book and realized she had plenty of content to fill 75% of her imagined book size based on their enthusiastic response. The main writing would be her telling her own story for the 25% remaining.

Dropped her negative beliefs and fears

Wrote her inspiring book of stories

HEALTHY WEIGHT

Every morning my client would get up in the morning and stand in the closet and endure a barrage of negative self-talk and self-loathing as she looked through the many sizes of clothes hanging in the closet, but could only fit into a few that were in the "big section," as she called it.

The amount of time in a day that she spent "longing to be thinner" and/or berating herself for eating something not on her diet was calculated at over 2.4 hours each day.

When she logged her time spent in this negative mind space, she was shocked by the amount of time. Naming the cost of her self-loathing was the fuel that fed her inner fire to shift.

In working with the *DROP IT* process, she began working through the high cost of what was running inside and got clear about what she was willing to do to have what she wanted. *remember Do NOT use the word lose, as the brain wants to gain. Focus on gaining health and ease.

AWARENESS and TRUTH

She recognized how much time and negative energy would be saved if she accomplished what she always wanted.

VISION

When she was her healthy weight, she felt what it would be like to walk into the closet filled with clothes in the size she desired and found that everything fit. She visualized herself cooking and eating healthy foods daily and dancing and walking with a friend thoroughly enjoying her new healthy body and positive view of herself.

She was able to reclaim that 2.4 hours and use it to take action to create the body she wanted and experience the powerful freedom, positivity, joy and ease she longed for.

LEGAL BATTLE

A client of mine had been swirling in the legal system fighting her ex to pay his fair share of child support. The Awareness phase revealed that she had spent 4 years and $55,000 dollars.

The Truth Telling phase revealed the huge amount of time, energy, focus and productivity that had been spent on having the same conversation about the drama she longed to end.

The Action phase led her to try one thing differently. She went to a free court lawyer who was not going to make money from her conflict. The lawyer looked through her legal filings and asked if her ex was working? She replied that he had not for over 10 years.

The lawyer looked her right in the eyes and said, "I'm sorry, but you're never going to see a dime of child support as long as he is not working, no matter how many millions of dollars he has in assets since the divorce. Child support is based on income."

My client was shocked, horrified and relieved. She could now choose to DROP IT, EMPTY OUT and get on with her life.

The battle to get him to pay and be fair.

The truth set her free to accept, harness time and find peace.

OWNING THE CALENDAR

A colleague of mine is a very seasoned coach and he was struggling to find time to write his next book. He had a full coaching practice of 24 clients and he charged them each month for 2 hours. He spent hours scheduling them and billing them each month.

I asked him what he ideally wanted: to increase his prices, create packages so he wouldn't have to bill so often and he would have chunks of time to just write and not be coaching.

NOTE: We can't make changes to create what we truly want if we are UNAWARE of new possibilities, information and resources that may allow us to achieve our desired outcome.

I shared the good news and truth: You can have an electronic calendar system for $15 a month that allows you to block off time for writing. If he wanted no more than 24 clients, he could actually block every other week off and his clients would be able to book into his open weeks in a 2-week cadence.

Even better, he would charge packages of time and they could book as often as they wanted using the electronic calendar which required no work on his part except to set it up and block off the time that he wanted to make available to his clients to book their own appts, or reschedule when necessary.

The tears of joy ran down his face when we walked through setting up his calendar system and he blocked off every other week so he could write and do whatever else he wanted in those weeks, while his clients had plenty of times open (including 3 hours on one Monday and 3 hours on one Friday of his off week's in case someone had to reschedule.).

He felt the relief and power of owning his calendar and having blocks of time for writing. By having packages, his hourly rate increased 30% and he saved more than 15 hours a month on scheduling and billing. He cried, "I own my life now."

If you want more choice, power, presence, inner peace, joy, vitality, health, freedom, a good night's sleep, productivity, focus, creativity, ease and more possibilities, practice **Drop It and Empty Out** and see what you experience next as the ripples create a new energy field inside you and all around you.

The practice becomes one of asking yourself on a regular basis, WHAT CAN I DROP that keeps me from having what I truly want and being productive, present and free for new possibilities?

This tool is something you can use and experiment with in every area of your work and life on any given day. And like every tool you have in your toolkit, it's only useful if you use it. Each time you go through this book, you may discover something you've been blind to.

Compassion and empathy are key when doing inner work.

Stay open and curious to what you truly want to be, do, have.

When you find yourself running things inside yourself that are robbing you of the present moment and the freedom you seek, take ACTION to unleash your productivity, presence and possibility.

DROP It and EMPTY OUT whatever needs to be released.

You Can Find Freedom, When You Take Action!

HARNESS TIME and FREE YOUR MIND

Organizations And Leaders Using Drop It To Create Thriving Cultures

Organizations are like any other system or community. It's a group of people who work together on behalf of an organized system. And each person broadcasts information into the environment creating either a thriving or surviving culture.

What is running inside your organization?

Trust Issues   Turnover Lack of Innovation

Meeting Fatigue   Burnout   Workplace Drama

What would be possible if people used *Drop It 2.0 and Emptied Out* old hurts, grudges, being passed over, and other things they are carrying?

What if people stopped having repetitive conversations?

What if people could give and receive feedback with ease?

What if leaders were broadcasting a different energy?

Maybe some of these are running inside your organization...?

fear of giving and receiving feedback

lack of resources and talent to balance work load

we've always done it this way, so why change

fear of making a mistake

talking about others to others

"They say things will change, but I don't believe it."

back-to-back meetings leaving no time to do work

toxic bosses and employees allowed to stay

Cultivating Efficiency

MEETING MANAGEMENT

Every day I hear people say, "I'm in back-to-back meetings and I can't get my work done during my 8-10 hour work day."

I hear executives telling me the same thing.

I'm amazed at the Victim responses I get as if no one (including the C Suite executives who run the company) have power to change meeting time spent. Really, all over the world I hear it.

Nothing changes until you make one shift.

Of those who have "tried" to shorten meetings, they say they get resistance. Isn't it interesting? Everyone complains about how many meetings they are in, but no one is willing to make them more efficient.

VICTIM or CREATOR

PERPETRATOR or CHALLENGER

Let me try moving from RESCUER to COACH here.

What's one thing you haven't tried to shorten and change the meeting culture in your company?

What beliefs do you have that you would have to let go of in order to create the outcome you desire?

When will you experiment with a new policy around meetings to create a more efficient workplace?

Imagine you have cut meeting times in half. What will you do with 50% more time? What growth could your company achieve when you have space to be doing productive innovation, strategic thinking or being more present to people to develop them?

Engagement and retention are serious challenges most organizations are facing in today's global environment.

Employees today know what they want from an employer and they are asking themselves questions like:

"Is this organization fully utilizing my gifts?

Do I feel valued here?

Does my work sustain me and make me happy?

Does my boss validate and inspire me?"

Opportunities for growth are also a major driver in managing talent and resources as global competition is fierce and affecting most industries.

New ways of working since 2020 are bringing fresh opportunities for companies to be innovative in all the ways people are working. Creating a thriving culture is evolving as the old ways of bringing people together are shifting.

A leader's ability to be present authentically and inspire their employees is a key factor in both engagement and retention.

Sustaining leaders in today's global economic environment is becoming more difficult given the extended work hours in most industries worldwide.

Companies want, need and have to be more innovative to stay competitive in the demanding, ever changing global market.

Organizations are now focusing their learning and development investments to teach self-coaching, leadership presence, resilience/stress management and managing attention.

The high cost of replacing talent is of grave concern and thus organizations are now focused on finding solutions to support sustainable leaders who can inspire and create environments that employees can enjoy and thrive in. Employees need to feel validated for their contributions. They want to make a difference.

We take ACTION when we have to. When the costs are too high not to.

Remember the research about productivity being directly related to the mood and presence of the boss?

How do companies create better moods in their leaders?

Helping everyone in an organization to learn to coach themselves so they thrive by shifting what is running inside that depletes their energy, focus and ability to be healthy, balanced and present at work is a good start.

When you reflect on how many things you identified that ran inside you, imagine how many things are actually running inside an organization when you tally each person. Workplace drama perpetuates a survival culture, not a thriving one.

Teams trying to work together with hidden grudges, resentments, past hurts or resignation can find it nearly impossible to sustain high performance for the long term.

And you can create and cultivate the thriving culture you want.

Our firm is committed to helping organizations and leaders master self-coaching and this Drop It 2.0 Tool to improve productivity, retention and engagement. Harness Time and Free Your Mind is one resource.

We also offer an on-demand course called *"Coach Your Self Up"* that teaches growth mindset, managing attention, career management skills, shifting self -limiting beliefs and deep stories that augment these tools and practices.

It is my hope that this book changes your life in unexpected ways!

May the power of your desire to HARNESS TIME and FREE YOUR MIND propel you to use these tools often and share them with others that you know and care about.

Peace, Presence, Health and Productivity to you and your organization!

Linda

Linda Newlin, MCC, is the founder and CEO of the Integrated Leadership Institute and Cultivate Talent Solutions. She has provided executive and team coaching, leadership development, search and training for over 30 years.

She brings a unique presence and professional breadth of experience from many industries and facets of change management, sustaining leaders, executive team development, coaching, on-boarding and recruiting to the clients she serves. Her tools and practices are grounded in the latest neuroscience to help create sustainable high impact change. Linda is a key note speaker.

She has worked with thousands of leaders and their teams at 3M, Microsoft, Unilever, PWC, Booz Allen, Nordson, Harvard, Danaher/Kavokerr, Merrill Lynch, T. Rowe Price, PacifiCare Health Systems, Genentech, Amgen, DuPont, Johnson & Johnson, Broadridge Financial, So Cal Gas, as well as many other companies and non-profits. She has also coached entrepreneurs and individuals around the world.

Linda is an ICF Master Certified Coach and Hudson Institute Certified Coach, with certifications in many assessments and tools to support clients. She has been a teacher for the Hoffman Institute, which provides a transformational process for individuals who are seeking to free themselves from past programming and become the source of change in their own lives. She co-created the *Inner Work of Leaders*, while on faculty.

She won the *Everyday Hero Award* from the Up With People Alumni Association for her commitment to helping children thrive through education and trauma recovery. Her music video called *It's Not Okay* is a powerful anti-abuse song produced to inspire change and healing.

Her passion for growth and transformation are reflected in all her work, books and music.

WFH: Working From Home: A Thrival Guide for Challenging Times and Beyond

> *"A must read for everyone!" – Marshall Goldsmith #1 NY Times Best-Selling Author*

The Inner Traveler's Guidebook to Moyo: Discovering the Power of Listening to Your Own Heart

> *"A beautiful, inspiring and unique healing musical journey to learn 16 self-loving practices" - Finola Hughes, Emmy award winning actor*

Growing Up Whole: A Child's Guide Book to Thriving

Being Whole: A Teen's Guide Book to Thriving

Living Whole: A Guide Book for Your Inner Child

> All artfully designed to draw, reflect and learn to practice valuable life skills: health, self-esteem, resilience, boundary setting, non-violent communication, compassion, validation, presence, naming emotions, positive thinking and visioning.

Also available are Companion *Validation Journal's* to build upon the practices and tools in each of the guide books.

GrowingUpWhole.com

Girl Dad gift booklet/card and all her music is available on:

Amazon.com (globally)

You Tube, Spotify, Apple Music, iTunes, etc.

Linda@CultivateTalentSolutions.com

We offer corporate discounts for volume purchases
of our books, on-demand Self Coaching Programs
And Customized Workshops for your Teams

Learn More About our Unique Approach and ROI

www.CultivateTalentSolutions.com

For More Information on Linda Newlin's
Other Books and Music
Please visit:

www.LindaNewlin.com

| More for Your Journey of Self-Coaching & Growth |

What Got You Here, Won't Get You There by Marshall Goldsmith

Coach Your Self Up by Mike Normant at the Unlimit Group
On-demand Course contact us CultivateTalentSolutions.com

Decisive Intuition by Rick Snyder at Invisible Edge
On-line Courses at Intuition University

Feedback Reimagined by Pete Berridge and Jen Ostrich

Take The Lead by Betsy Myers

Testimonials

*"**HARNESS TIME and FREE YOUR MIND** changed my life and my organization. I stopped thinking like a victim and took action to create meetings that last 15 minutes. We have separate social times to connect, which are more enriching than ever." TK*

"Your masterful coaching helped me to create the life I wanted. I received so much more from our coaching engagement than I had expected. I have worked with other coaches, but clearly your experience, knowledge of neuroscience and behavior change and presence are unique. The changes are incredible." DH

"You are a compass for the wandering soul. Using the Empty Out Tool changed my energy so quickly I was in disbelief for days afterwards. Having been fired the day before Christmas 3 years ago I was still carrying so much baggage inside. This simple tool literally brought my freedom and MOJO back. THANK YOU! – PM

"Your presence and expertise are a magical combination. I could not have imagined getting all that I got from our work together."

"My transition and successful integration in this new management role was made possible because of your expert coaching and transition work with me and my team during these past 6 months. Thank you for all your support." - G Smith

"I never would have considered working with a coach before to help me make changes I was trying to make. But you were highly recommended…and now I know why. So many things I've always wanted have manifested and are working in my life. Thank you so much for helping me create sustainable change." KMurphy

"Our organization has created a coaching culture where people are harnessing time and developing themselves using your tools and the Coach Your Self Up™ course content in powerful ways for managing their own career growth. Thank you!" - RJ

Made in the USA
Middletown, DE
19 September 2023

38796365R00089